ROUGH

Also by Nathalie Anderson:

Following Fred Astaire
Crawlers
Quiver
Held and Firmly Bound
Stain

ROUGH

Nathalie Anderson

THE WORD WORKS

Rough © 2024 Nathalie Anderson

◊

Reproduction of any part of this book
in any form by any means,
electronic or mechanical,
must be with permission
in writing from
the publisher.
Address
inquiries to:
The Word Works
P.O. Box 42164
Washington, D.C. 20015
editor@wordworksbooks.org

Cover Design: Susan Pearce Design
Cover Art: Randall Exon
Author Photo: JPG Photography and Video

◊

Library of Congress Control Number: 2024934730
International Standard Book Number: 978-1-944585-75-4

Acknowledgments

Thanks to the following journals and anthologies, where these poems have previously appeared:

Big Bridge: "Roots"
Cold Mountain Review: "Omens"
Fox Chase Review: "Beauty," "Campus," "Cold Hands," "Concourse," "Lawn Boys," and "Rough"
Irish Studies South: "Somebody's Saints March In"
Jasper: "Crêche"
Natural Bridge: "Mystery" and "Celebrity"
Veterans for Peace Newsletter: "Berlin, Belfast, Belgrade, Baghdad, Basra"
Nimrod International Journal: "Rapture" (semi-finalist, Pablo Neruda Prize for Poetry)
On Barcelona: "Autumn, Casa Batlló"
The Philadelphia Inquirer: "Poll"
Small Craft: "Rant"
The Swarthmorean: "Catch," "Inked," "The Veiling," and *"Zueignung"*

Anthology of Featured Poets: Moonstone Poetry Series: "Berlin, Belfast, Belgrade, Baghdad, Basra"
Art Through the Eyes of Mad Poets: An Ekphrastic Poetry Collection: "Trouble" and "Annunciation / Denunciation"
Open-Eyed, Full-Throated: An Anthology of American/Irish Poets: "King of the Cats," "Reunion," and "Rough"
The Plume Anthology of Poetry: "Dead Doll" (2017) and "Afghan Rug," published as "Victorian Dreaming" (2013)
Poetry Ink: 20th Anniversary Anthology: "Minding the White Horse"

"Sad Sacks" was originally included in *Secret Heart*, a chapbook of 17 poems, selected for on-line excerpted publication through the University of South Carolina Poetry Initiative Chapbook Series.

"Crazy" and "Minding the White Horse" are from a series of eight poems commissioned for the "Frisson" artists' program of the Columbia, S. C., Museum of Art.

I am grateful to Swarthmore College for support in completing this manuscript, and to Karren Alenier, Abbe Blum, Betsy Bolton, Michaelyn Burnette, Joy Charlton, Gregory Djanikian, Major Jackson, Nzadi Keita, Kathryn Kirkpatrick, David Lloyd, Ed Madden, Lisa Sewell, Kristina Straub, Elaine Terranova, Terry Tierney, JC Todd, Eamonn Wall, Lesley Wheeler, Nancy White, and Thomas Whitman for encouragement and advice.

Thank you to Randall Exon for the cover art and to Susan Pearce for the design.

Contents

    Rough / 3

I   Don't Look Back: Three Orphean Fables / 7
    Rant / 10
    Beauty / 12
    The Librarian / 14
    Grave Goods / 15
    the vanishing / 21
    King of the Cats / 23

II   Trouble / 27
    Annunciation / Denunciation / 28
    Minding the White Horse / 30
    Cavalry Maneuvers, Camp de Châlons, 1857 / 31
    Afghan Rug / 32
    Crazy / 33
    Sad Sacks: Wartime Photos, Home Front / 34
    Clair-obscur / 38

III   Rapture / 41
    Crêche / 46
    Strong Man / 47

IV   Still / 55

V   Fresh Air / 63
    Inked / 64
    Omens / 65
    Lawn Boys / 66
    Reunion / 68
    Practicing Old / 69
    Poll / 70
    Concourse / 72
    Cold Hands / 73
    Roots / 74
    Veiling / 75
    Catch / 76

VI	Dead Doll / 79
	Show Runner / 81
	Mystery / 82
	Celebrity / 84
	Glass Beach / 86
	Englands of the Mind / 88
	Autumn, Casa Batlló / 89
	Somebody's Saints March In / 91
	Berlin, Belfast, Belgrade, Baghdad, Basra / 93
VII	Four Snow Moans / 97
	Zueignung / 99

Notes / 101
About the Author / About the Artist / 103
About The Word Works / 104
Other Word Works Books / 105

In memory:

AV Christie, Linda DelVecchio, Anne Garrison, Nade Haley,
Janet Kaplan,
Joan Landis, George Moskos

Rough

After the sightings, the sea got rough,
got rough on us, shale fallen to scarp and
shoving down, shunting against itself,
scathing and carping, flints striking flakes
off each other, sparking white, black, white.

Did I say sightings? I meant to say biting.
Nobody in beyond the ankle but
still that slash to the ankle bone, the sea
a susurrus of open-jawed serration,
strange voice at your ear.

Whatever we glimpsed out there hid itself
in potentia, flexing its muscle
under the water's skin. Head of a hawk,
head of a rottweiler. And the seals
in their slickers, black-backed, menaced

as we were, too doggish to know it. Her husband
lost like that, no longer the man she'd married,
but when were we ever? Nail head. Hammer head.
When will you admit you didn't know your own mother?
Strange mouth at your ear. Strange hand on your arm.

And did I say spiky? I meant to say spiny.
We could feel it under foot, every step
from the shoreline to the car. The sand
rough on us, the mind rougher.
Cross-cut saw. Shredder.

I

Don't Look Back: Three Orphean Fables

1. The Cage

Don't look back, she told herself, leaving hell
for heaven, stumbling over her own feet
those first steps out of the cage, fearing less
to feel again the acid scoriations
than to see for sure the paltry bounds
they'd held her: the latch that any other child
might easily have lifted, the meager shelf
of meager books, the grit they fed her,
filth they set her sorting.

Yet those first weeks at college found her yearning,
though for the life of her she couldn't see what for –
some shape of things impossible? some shadowy savior?
the reassuring weight of the accustomed chain?

Don't tell. Don't dwell in it. Don't fester.
The world restores itself, wants reconciliation,
not recrimination. *Don't look*: she never.
Still, dreams twist her nightly back into that
little bed of cinders, and every morning
she steps up, ready to spill the beans.

2. The Name

Don't look back: he lived like that, striding
ever forward, stepping through trouble
like he'd shed a pair of pants, the kind of guy
a girl can't help but follow. *That's one to keep
your eyes on*, gossips said, but did they mean
so to track him like a meteor, that glitter, or
so to mark him for a snake? Even in the back-water
back-woods back-of-beyond, she'd heard tell how
he'd talk the birds from the trees, the tabby
off the cat, wheat from chaff, curds from whey, the dead
up out of the grave – though how he managed, she

couldn't for the life of her see: no back-slaps, no
back-scratch, no back-handed push-backs – just him,
best-selling, critically acclaimed. Did he know
how close she shadowed him? always back-drop
to his bright stage. Of course there was back-lash –
back-biters' back-talk, back-seat back-pedaling – but
(don't look back) he never. If he'd once turn his head
she'd be there – his back-up, his back-bone – but
as it was, *I've got your back* she'd whisper
to his blind obliviousness, matching his stride,
mapping his territory, gripping the knife.

3. The Shade

Don't look back: such good advice, and so he never –
never the what-if, never the why-whine. Yet
then heard first the doubled step, the faintest
paso doble, like your steps might stutter
through a tunnel, like your shadow might slip on heels
to heel you. The little hairs at the nape of his neck
rose up as though of their own accord, rose up
as though breathed through, his quick pulse quickening
the canon of his own breathing, the echoing breath
almost a noise, almost a voice, like someone
talking soft long after dark in the farthest room
of the neighboring apartment. Every word
now said seemed overheard, seemed tested, tasted,
scrutinized. The pain in the neck, the tap
on the shoulder – say, when the rains first fell –
came now so intimate: a stroke of luck,
a fate, a shadowing. While he slept,
did he dream something circling
his wrist, his waist, his ankle, almost
a scent, almost a sensing?

And thus he came to understand death's bargain,
the trade he'd made for the life of her:
Don't look back. Don't look back once, and she'd be still his –
his back-of-your-mind, his under-your-skin, his ever-more.

Rant

Practicing all morning every morning
for a week before the wake, practicing
hard, repeating myself, speaking over
and over my small spliff of consolation,
in shower, by mirror, in larder, by
heart, and every time making myself cry

with poetry. Hating myself for how
my voice cracks, grief sloshing out in gasps and gusts.
Hate how I shake, deep tremor, after-shocks.
Hate how flash it comes, and out of nothing:
rip tide, dry lightning. Hate how words do this
so fast I look soft, cheap, mawkish, easy.

Whose poem? Not that it matters much, but
this time it's Millay. I hate her, too, for how
from words that could mean anyone at all –
"the intelligent, the witty, the brave" –
I see my friend, his beard grown hermit-wild,
his eyes still glacier-blue, lifting his hand

to his breast bone, saying "what I feel now
is the world's pain, the essential pain: both
essence of pain, and essential to me. I
don't want to feel, yet feel I need to feel it."
Where's he gone, that man who danced like the wind
and thought like he danced? And where's that woman

whose eyebrows always almost met, who
crinkled when she smiled? Or that woman who
ruled the roost like a banty cock? Or that man
with the nervous foot, the over-anxious heart?
Is this essential pain? I want my friends.
I want Allen. Linda. Joan. George. Janet.

O double-dealer, you with the shell-game,
the bait-and-switch, the predatory loan,
who one by one takes back each gracious gift
you give, I hope you're reading this. Out loud.
In public. Before witnesses. Read it
again and again, why don't you? Read it and weep.

Beauty

To see her as I first saw her: her hair
a dark cloud, her brow a dark echo, and
something about the eyes: a freckling? Once

I thought her pregnant when she was not: that
rootedness, flat-footedness, air moving
around her, never disarranging her

and lit like a lantern from within she
took no offense: slightly puzzled, slightly
amused: her smile bemused and generous. If

beauty is the face that glows for us, why
crave so the aloof, the reserved, the eye
that refuses? Yet she was both: open, closed;

homely and exotic; unembroidered
yet elegant. Something about the eyes:
a scintillation? As she was dying, she

explained even that: calmly, kindly: a mathematician's
enumerations. *Don't you think*, she'd start to ask, and
you'd think *yes*. When beauty walks through your life,

how do you talk with it, how do you speak
through its pregnant pauses? A tree that moves
its branches slowly. Why one face draws us

and another leaves us cold: when do we
stumble into this discrimination? The last time
I saw her blends into every other:

dark stroke of hair, dark stroke of brow, dark stroke
of mouth: a chiaroscuro portrait. Something
about the eyes: a rimpling? No one

whom crow's feet so complimented. The quick shock
of her laugh. And me still in awe of her
beauty, so unselfconsciously she wore it.

The Librarian

Where does it go, that erudition,
when the scholars shrug off their doubts, shrug
into their cloaks, their intuitions,
when the carrels furl shut and the doors
click closed behind them? Where does it go
as night falls hard and the wind flies high,
when the only light is the moon's light
through window, scrim of snow, drifted snow
and snow bank? Following one who could
put a hand to any given book
in the pitch dark, knowing the shelves so
by heart. *Ubi sunt?* Where does it go?

We're in her archive now, where every book
is an open book, and every page so
intricately made, we'll never
read the end of it. See how the moon
sighs, rests her hand on the desk,
rests her cheek in her hand? See
how the wind shelves and reshelves
straight through to dawn? How with all the time
in the world, the snow keeps turning
and turning its white pages? Where
does it go – O bright skies, O wind-blown air! –
all that time, all our time in the world?

Grave Goods

1. Packed for the Afterlife
    – *reading* Archaeology *magazine*

The coffin like a steamer trunk, the body
rolled up tight and tucked to one side, leaving
ample space for garments, goods. Of course you'll pack
the gossamer, the gold brocade, the furs. Layers!
What can be padded on, what can be stripped away –
who knows if you'll be cold or hot, who knows
who you might be meeting. And of course you'll take
your sky shoes, the bronzed uppers lacy so the air
can breeze through, the soles gilded with cloud, with flame,
and spiked for easy climbing. And your silver hands –
de rigueur in polite circles, the handshakes
more elegant, the ensemble more discreet....

Way too many opportunities, it's true,
for pilfering, the deceased preoccupied
otherwise and elsewhere, the attendants so
discerning. Who can say if this is *really*
the best bone flute, the best gold torc, the very best
of the broken china they've wrapped efficiently
in sashes, headscarves, shifts, slips, skirts, linens? Some
avoid the problem altogether by packing
the attendants, too – and such a help, once you've
arrived. I can't begin to tell what some folks
carry: whole boats, horses, miniature houses,
little farms for future snacking, signets, cats,

armies. A word of caution: colors fade out
over time, and fabrics fray, and moths corrupt,
so pack wisely – you won't want to be wearing
shreds in perpetuity. And dust sifts in
despite best precautions. I knew a lady
from Jiangsu Province whose entire wardrobe –
all her silks and damasks – turned in transit to
deep ochre, slightly brickish, rust-tinged, her hems

(the most exposed part) blackened as if dragged in dirt.
And as for her celebrated embroideries—
rustling grasses, meadow flies, fireflies, dragonflies—
frankly, who can tell anymore what's what?

I know fashion's changed. You'd be lucky these days
to voyage out in half a suit. But consider
all your options. For a start, the ennui - it'll
seem like eternity for sure without a book
or deck of cards, a chess set or companion
to divert and entertain you. Take your spouse?
And no telling what the shops are like, what
currency they're cashing. My friend from Jiangsu
stitched silver round her collars, gold up her sleeves.
Some think to sell their souls. Some think they'll be fine
with nothing in their hands - but would you stand naked
there where you don't know anyone yet, or worse, where you do?

2. The Most Toys

That summer on Cape Cod, my friend Janet and I
spent a full afternoon at a mid-scale boutique
where she tried on every scrap in the shop, assembling
ensembles for a trip to Turkey. She knew just
what she wanted: to look professional, to seem
modest, to stay crisp despite the heat, to project
every kind of cool – she was headed over to
curate artists' installations in Turkish jails.
Separates, she figured, and – just like that – bought three
or four pairs of pants, maybe twice that many tops,
all of them co-ordinating edgily. Wow.
I was entirely impressed, especially because

I am myself a magpie purchaser. So many
thrift store finds scintillate on my hangers but don't
quite harmonize. That geometric black and white
I've worn just once, to my niece's wedding. The blue brocade
just once, for a fancy-schmancy concert. The handkerchief hem –
passé an hour after I'd bought it, but I can't let it go, can't
let any of it go. When my step-mother down-sized,
she filled the dining room table with jelly glasses,
some chipped, some cracked through; told us, "surely you children
can get some more use out of these." In the retirement village,
she kept a storage locker packed floor to ceiling with gifts
she'd bought us on spec over time, and every one a bargain.

The curious keep curios; comics collect comic books in bales.
My brother's filled an upright architect's file
with vintage Audubon prints he can't get to, since
every inch of his floor's jam-packed. For me, it's books
stacked high to toppling, my own best insulation. Raised
as children by children of the Great Depression, we
learned early to accumulate. That summer on Cape Cod,
Janet rented a furnished place with what she called
the Tomb Room, so full it was with the landlord's artifacts: mirrors,

vases, tea chests, trophies, pillows, rolled rugs, dictionaries, globes,
ships in bottles, golf clubs, broken clocks, dead lamps –
some of it enticing, most of it scrap. Grave goods. As she shrank

down to nothing in the months before her going, Janet
bought herself a whole new wardrobe, gloried
in tight sweaters, skinny jeans. I wish I had her eye,
wish I knew where her every shop might be. Once
at the Penn Museum of Anthropology and Archaeology,
we spent a full forty-five minutes handling every textile
heaped high by a vendor of Japanese stencil work. Intent,
methodical, she knew what she wanted: not svelte elegance,
quirky elegance. She bought scraps of that cloth
to frame for friends in Byzantium, Nineveh, Luxor. We
had lunch, strolled among the hieroglyphics and sarcophagi.
"Who has the most toys?" she'd joke, and I'd answer "Tut."

3. Visitations

The dead come back so seldom, we
forget how to please them. That one time,
for me, for instance, my lost man did all
the heavy lifting: I mean there
he was, waiting patient for me
to catch on, catch up to him, then
there he wasn't. Now I'm wracked:
what fell thing did I do by chance
to open that door, invite him in –
clipped what nail or hair or shirt? slipped
what under plate or pillow, feather
say or fern? and was there blood let –
paper cut? bit lip? I'd do it again, but

you can't waste their time: what you saw,
what you said, what you wore – that's
nothing to them now. Used to be,
I'd bring the show-and-tell: the books,
the snaps, the toys, the news, the drafts
I thought she'd like – but what's to bring
now she knows all? Used to be, I'd
leave her ticket with the usher, she'd
run so far behind. That last time,
she missed the film, met me after
at the parking garage, leaning –
I'd like to say insouciant –
against a bollard, face blue though

and her lips puce, couldn't lift
her own legs into the cab but
still sent back the mushy shrimp, still
waxed crucially sardonic, still
turned every page of that Jack Yeats,
still shook up all I brought her. That one time,
minding my father – he was gone
already, would stay gone like that

another seven years – I laid
this out: how, from the air, over
the leafless woods, from Pennsylvania
south to Carolina, the noon sun

caught the streams: who knew how many?
a tangled skein of silver. I
don't think he even turned his head.
Maybe I was air to him, or
trickling water? No wonder
he never comes to visit. But
who knows what they'll come for. Likely
not my sorry-for-myself, my
"every place in this city you
might name, we were there together,"
my snuffling in concerts, my
wail in the driveway. No way she'd
stand still five minutes for that shit
(or this), my late late friend.

the vanishing

what can I say
you fell from my hand
I was looking aside
I was looking askew

I left you behind
it happened that fast
I flung out my hand
you flew who knows where

like my bank card at heathrow
like my sweet turquoise ring
you fell from my hand
I felt nothing at all

I retraced my steps
kept my eyes to the ground
half the bankers in Philly
knew my loss before me

my sweet turquoise ring
I bought for myself
when I was thirteen
you were with me that long

I flung out my hand
my fingers had thinned
I shook back my hair
you slipped down the drain

rain falling on water
mist rising to air
ice melting to nothing
like that you were spent

how could I not know
when you ran out of heart
I turn up my palms
what line have I cropped

in brooklyn you fell
at heathrow, at home
I was walking along
I was looking away

I was counting my cash
I was counting my rings
like god counting his sparrows
I was counting on air

King of the Cats

1. Who's Pavarotti now there's no Pavarotti?
   Who's the new Yeats, now there's no more Yeats?
   What was it Yeats said when Swinburne passed?
   He said it to his sister. "Now I'm the king of the cats."

2. Once Caesar's stabbed, who bullies round the capital?
   Twenty men on the ballot, all angling to be Lincoln.
   Who crossed that river? Who swung that axe?
   When the oak's brought down, every shrub looks tall.

   And if we cloned Genghis Khan, would the new Khan
   sweep through Asia? Would he cry - with Yeats - "Let all things
   pass away"? The wind through the forum blows hot and cold.
   "There come now no kings nor Caesars," wrote Pound, pre-Mussolini.

3. What was it the spirit communicators said
   when Yeats thought his one first child might be enough?
   They said, "Your daughter's birth prepares the way." They said,
   "Your boy will alter time and times." They said

   "O Solomon! Let us try again!" They spoke thus
   through the mouth of Mrs. Yeats. While scholars debate
   the implications, in the audience Michael Yeats - that very boy -
   holds his head in his hands - for all his birth and honors,
           not that child.

4. Is Caruso's son born singing, or born silenced? Imagine the strained
   anticipation of his every burble and squeak. Can he, will he
   follow along? Or consider the grandchild writing school essays
   on her famous kin. Does she say what she knows for true - Gran

   told me *this* - or hide what she doesn't? - arcane knowledge
   or baffled incomprehension held equally close to the chest.
   Natalie Cole, Sean Lennon, Jacob Dylan, Priscilla Presley.
   The one thing they'll never do is sing just like their fathers.

5. "Funny thing," says the man, home late from the pub. The wife
    looks dubious, strokes their drowsing tabby. "Just now," says the man,
    "a cat crossed my path, then another, and another –
    twelve cats in all – till the last, this itty bitty kitten, says

    Tell Tam Skattermiwaul! Tam Skattermiwaul has died." You can guess, the
    who springs from the hearth, whose hair bristles out, who capers,
          who jigs,
    who flies round the room and right up the chimney. You can guess
    what's shouted, what's screeched. You can guess who's left
          open-mouthed.

6. The Norton anthology, which footnotes even
    Eve and Adam, footnotes Yeats too, in Auden's elegy. Paquin
    once gowned the lithest socialites. Now she's a footnote to Pound's
    Pisan cantos, and no one says her name or wears her brand. Who's
          Pavarotti,

    my students asked last week. Who's Yeats? Who's Pound?
    "Gone with the wind," writes Dowson, "between the kisses
          and the wine."
    Who's Dowson? Who remembers? Something's tapping at the tables,
    something's dragging at the pen, maybe it's Yeats himself

7. but who's to know? There's no Yeats left to listen,
    no Pavarotti left to sing. Who's the new
    Pavarotti? I can't think who.
    My friends, there are no friends.

II

Trouble

– after The Annunciation, *Henry Ossawa Tanner, 1898*

1. My bed looks just like that
   when I've wrestled myself all night –
   A shed skin. A convulsing.

2. Does my face look like that, too,
   facing the light? Hands gripped so hard
   you forget the twisted arm.

3. Caught out between a shudder
   and a tremble. Some choices,
   you can't say no to, can't say yes.

4. Wouldn't any girl look just like that
   as she takes it in, the word
   that redefines her?

5. The word
   she didn't ask
   to redefine her.

Annunciation / Denunciation

– *after* The Annunciation, Henry Ossawa Tanner, 1898

The family account ... reports that Sarah [Tanner's mother] ... was one of eleven children born to a slave named Elizabeth. Six of Elizabeth's children were fathered by Charles Miller, a freedman who wanted to marry her; five of her children were fathered by the slave master who owned the plantation. Each time Miller saved enough money to purchase Elizabeth's freedom, the slave master increased the price. Finally Elizabeth contacted agents of the Underground Railroad. With their assistance, she put Sarah and her other children in one of the master's double-team wagons, stocked it with food, and sent them away at midnight, never to see them again.

– Rae Alexander-Minter, "The Tanner Family: A Grandniece's Chronicle," *Henry Ossawa Tanner*, ed. Dewey F. Mosby, Philadelphia Museum of Art and Rizzoli, 1991.

1. Henry Tanner's mother
was born halved, her two skins,
yolk and cream,
curdled into each other –
or so I imagine.

Henry's mother's mother
whisked her right out of there
with the other ten children
coddled low in the straw
to hide what was hatching.

No hen for their henhouse –
six children the husband's,
five children the master's,
all of them owned and owed,
if they'd been uncovered.

2.   Away in a manger
     I imagine her there
     Henry's mother's mother
     laid down in the dark
     no choice in the matter.

     Five times at least, the light
     in the doorway, the stars
     in the bright sky, the strength
     of his arm. Lowliness. Dung.
     No crying she makes.

     The handmaid of the lord.
     According to thy word.
     Hunched almost into cower,
     eyes staring out from under –
     what now do you see here?

3.   Henry Tanner's mother
     named him Ossawa, for
     Osawatomie, Kansas, where
     John Brown launched himself
     towards Harper's Ferry.

     Tanner painted his mother
     like Whistler's mother –
     same pose, but human.
     The commentator praises
     his "relaxed geometries."

     I imagine her there –
     Tanner's mother's mother –
     packing her children off
     at midnight in that wagon.
     Whose soul doth magnify?

Minding the White Horse

    – *after George Biddle's painting* South Carolina Landscape

Every last bush here is dark at its heart,
parched and yellowed at its rim. The cabin cants,
the porch pole leans, and the tar-paper's thin
over the rafters, mossy where the rain pools between.
Every last field is stumped and stubbled, the sand
sifting over the red clay. Nothing easy grows here.

So that's what he grazes: crops the dry grass
down to the dirt, mumbles the stubble, mouths up
thistles and stickers. His neck's half to giraffe
from reaching, his shoulders stubborn as the fields
we plow. He's always jawing. You can't shoo him.

And mouth to mouth, he thins and thins. Our land
alters him, the red earth rusting along his spine,
moss furrowing under each rib. His back
dips like our roof beam. His tail's a bony memory.

Haste! Haste! Something's rising, storming the horizon –
the mule's ears blown forward, the mule's tail blown
between his legs, the shutter slamming shut and open.

The white horse stands pat, thunder in his eye. He knows
who'll be riding him, who'll be riding him

soon.

Cavalry Maneuvers, Camp de Châlons, 1857

– after a photograph by Gustave Le Gray

1.
Caught edging the line where dark outfaces light,
where earth squares off against the sky, these horsemen
constitute our horizon. Beyond them
we can't see. A grove of soldiers, high-horsed
and high-hatted, pruned all to the same height,
so disciplined their silhouettes stand sentry still.

2.
Nothing like, of course, from where they sit their saddles.
Each man's his own center. Stark sky, black plain extend
around beyond him, vista-vast on every side,
and the far hills – no indeterminate smudge – arrest
and rest his eye with gold, red, violet, green. Leather creaks
and horse-hair bristles. Underneath his uniform

he chafes, he sweats, he itches. Needs to piss. Flies blurt
up from the horse-shit to nip at his neck, and you can bet
he curses, last night's cheese and garlic thickening
his tongue. A toggle's loose on his jacket, the flashed braid
fast unraveling, and he's counting on his fingers,
thinking *hélas*, thinking *combien*. Girls like him, like

the uniform, the felted serge of it again today
soaked through with sweat that stiffens as it chills.
Maneuvers: his turn's coming. The horse beneath him
quivers, whickers. Under the massed fur of his hat
the hair's matted flat and likely lousy. Before him
the cadre wheels, halts. Chalk pounds up, dusty as a schoolroom.

3.
Eight horsemen to the left maneuver smartly. Twenty
to the right stand fast at fixed attention. Two officers
direct, observe, review. Not one of them can see
what's coming for them. Rout or pyrrhic victory.
Dysentery, cholera. Bullet, bayonet, or bomb.
The trenches. Occupation. Algeria. Dien Bien Phu.

One hundred fifty years gone by and each its own
disaster. They have no idea we're watching them
knowing what we know. But look: at the center there
some scout, some message boy or loose lieutenant, turning
his back on black and white divisions, hazes off forever
beyond our capability to imagine him.

Afghan Rug

I figure it thus: a man stands all night
at a stand-up desk, stands figuring. Sums
scratched to foolscap scraps, snatched up, scattered – he
scarcely notices, his fair-hand crab-crawling
the brass-bound ledger, cross-copying out
meticulous accounts – best copperplate,
best boilerplate, each seven and zed crossed twice
for elegance, each g and y descending
into flourishings. Cuts quite the figure: sleeves
banded back and the cuffs scuffed to fraying,
wrists scrubbing the desk's edge till both patina,
cheek smudged where for a moment he propped it
dotting subtly the splattered blotter,
and the back straining tall, the weight shifted
hip to hip, the thighs clenched, the calves cramping,
even the arches braced against their fall,
eyes opened so long in ghastly gaslight
he thinks he sees beneath his feet the carpet writhe.

And writhe it does, what with the moths mating –
that twitch, that wing-throb – and the eggs hatching out –
that shuddering lather – and the maggots
urgent, pale pulsing slugs, each swallowing
its thread, gnawing it down to its nub; knots
unknotted – figure that! – strand by strand through
the deep-dyed wool; the bold geometries
and arabesques turned tatty, threadbare; and
all knitted, knotted back in tight cocoons, tinged
each with hints of former hues, the rose blanched,
the gold gone sallow, blue ashen, lilac
a dusky shadow. So at night's end, when
they open to the flit and tizzy of
new-hued moths, it's a knot garden rising,
a haze exotic in the air, before
he turns to look, and it all unravels.

Crazy

> – *after Flora Hannah Lott's quilt*

Any lumberjack can fit you up your
snug log cabin. Any fool can turn you
down the drunkard's path. I sew what I see,
sew what I know. I can give you beetles.
I can give you scissors. I can give you
wide-eyed owls in the deadest midnight tree.

Any farmer's wife can arrow through your
fleetest flying geese. Any preacher's wife
can polish off your rich cathedral window.
Furrow, fallow. I can give you nation
feather-stitched to nation. I can give you
the black cloth rubbing up against the white.

Christmas star, broken star, wandering star –
it takes a wise woman not to follow.
I can give you soft. I can give you sour.
Goats in the posies. Flags flown upside down.
Pea pods. Poppies. Peacock feathers.
Fuchsia. About fifty other flowers.

Any good sailor can navigate your
storm at sea. Any good weaver can lace
your spider's web. I can give you eagles
nesting in velvet, frogs swimming in silk.
Cats and anchors. Horse-shoes. Guitars. I can
give you the bride with tears ripped down her face.

Sad Sacks: Wartime Photos, Home Front

– after a photograph album kept during World War II by Elize Hodges

1.
Sad Sacks: Perhaps you've seen the comic strip, first drawn
by George Baker in *Yank* (the Army weekly)
in 1942: a doofus GI trips repeatedly, perpetually,
on every military irony. Fed through the '50s
on leftover rations, choking back each glutinous bite, I
sympathize especially with his strip on spam: slapped with it, splatted
meal after meal in the mess, in the field, the Sad Sack
opens eagerly the package from home, of course to find

more spam: two thick and oozing bricks of it. Sad Sacks:
fatigues designed inevitably to sag, scut work devised
inexorably to sap, the assy brass deployed
insidiously for sassing but impervious to sass –
defeat before the battle, attrition from mere circumstance,
the under-belt of bravery, the banal cheek of sacrifice.
Three-quarters through an album kept in the midst of war, it's no surprise
Miss Elize Hodges titles a two-page photo spread "Sad Sacks" –

though everybody here appears civilian: girls proud
as ramrods; guys with carefully combed hair; each skirt
and tennis dress and pinafore bleached out, blinding; each flirt
with his sleeves rolled; bow ties, white jackets; a guy with a sweet mouth;
a girl, her chin tucked, ducking a joke; tossed heads, turned heads –
slim slips and blots of light, with all outdoors behind them: lakes
barely rippling, hillsides of houses, swagged evergreens; three friends
in a forest, two dressed for a dance; arrays of blaze and shade

and every snapshot torn from its matrix, stripped to its essence,
ripped back to its core: rough deckling framing the raised arm, skimming
away the hair line; neat rectangles scumbled, rounded, slimming
further the slender girls, turning the town boys rugged. Innocence,
irreverence: a couple flanking a tiered fountain, only their heads left, askew;
a bridesmaid, bouqueted and banqueted, shoulders bared, head gone –
everyone anonymous, piled on the page: rough-edged river rocks set in a wall –
the only man conceivably in uniform standing steady, stalwart, in a
      canted canoe.

2.
SAD SACKS: the letters spelling out this title, too, she's torn –
Miss Elize Hodges – from portraits of herself: the flirty snap
on the hood of the car, the sweet study in the white pinafore,
a block of teacher pictures in prim-collared blouse, the striped dress
vined with nosegays, the frilled dress with the tucked smocked bodice,
the letters' torn edges just skirting her skirts, just raising her hems,

so the two As flare with her hair, open to her shoulders,
widen for her hip, her legs angled artfully down the one A,
the snipped-out space in the letter's center opening there
like a Mason's eye, eclipsing most of the face; where in the other A
it's slitting the dress, stinging, a little lethal dart. One S swerves
with the curve of her cheek, masking the eyes, spotlighting the smile; while

one S snakes past her torso, scaling the trim waist, the braceleted arm;
and one S raises a leafy canopy over a fallen frock, the shaded shoulders
and the bent head pared away. The well of the D has swallowed all
but belly and sleeve; while of the twinned teachers, the K's upper arm
shows half a mouth, and the lower only an eye, a stray puff of hair.
Meanwhile, at the beach, the sky's white, the sand's white, the sea a grey bar,

two ankles showing dark in the C's lower jaw.

3.
Why "Sad Sacks"? Oh, come on now. You tell me.
Here's the green wood, here's the working farm,
where every face is sunlit. Was any smile
ever so guileless, any eye so blithe?

Wheeling a bike down the brick stoop. The back
half-turned in the rowboat. Every face nameless.
Girls with their hands poised, one over the other,
the Vs of their arms like checkmarks down the page.

Camp cabin, stones stepped steep before it,
dug back deep in the dirt, yet every boat's
precarious. She lifts her hand to cup a blossom
and the world swirls around her.

Winds whine in the pines. Tunes
spume off the radio. *Et in Arcadia
Ego*. Whose voice are you listening for
here in the heart of our own war?

Clair-obscur

– after a photograph by Gustave Le Gray, Études de nuages

High moon and scumbled cloud –
Who claims the night goes dark?
Some subtlety moving still
over the face of the deep.

Slip off into lisp and whisper,
into undertone and moan.
Every slow wave breaks
with your father's voice.

Who's plumbed
those starkest waters?
What's that you say?
Every lost last word

flung back at you.
What's that you hear
in the deep choke and chuckle
under the lip of the sea?

III

Rapture

> *"...only a toy-box version of the Apocalypse."*
> *– Jonathan Kirsch,* A History of the End of the World

1. Sister
> *"Till God burn nature with a kiss"*

I was caught in a kiss: that's how – but not
"caught out," not like ma's sharp shaming, more like
"caught up," like something vast reached down to grab
and raise me by the hair. Bible camp, me
hot to be saintly, picking up rubbish
in the outdoor chapel, tracking the sun
row to row down the plank pews, head tilted
just so, face exalted, haloed hair, and
nobody to see it, just like at school
where beauty's blessed with beauty, and no one
else can win. Yeah, I'm the shunned one, the stone
the sorry builder always passes by.

And that smug crowd past dinner hopped so high
on righteousness I had to get out, back
to my own – what? – loner devotionals,
ducking from their dazzle into the pitch black
back of the closed canteen, inching, halting,
walking blind – benighted – when just like that
the rush, the grip, the swing, the dip, the rush.
He opened my mouth to his and filled it,
left me gasping, like icy water when
you don't yet know you're thirsty, like water
when you don't yet know you're parched, and I thought
I'm no stone. I am the lily of the fields.

Who was it? Next day, believe me, I spied
close at every face. No one looked different,
or looked at me different, or even looked
at me at all. A mystery. Silence
in heaven. I've kissed since then, kiss after kiss –

bad boys who'll kiss anyone, good boys who
kiss for thrills. Pa threatens, ma despairs, but
now I know what I know: there's nothing like.
When I think of that kiss I thirst so deep
I'm staggered, swept off my feet. O angels!
Messengers! I'm sealed, sealed and delivered,
rapt for the rapture, sealed with His kiss.

2. Brother

"Terrible swift sword"

Kapow he's down. Kablam he stands. No beast
prevails against him. The seven hells
can't hold him. That's Jesus. That's my man.

Wars and rumors of wars. Copters and humvees.
He smites them, rapid fire. He trumpets
up a storm. Zwoom. That's his incoming arm.

And he tramples out the grapes of wrath. The heads
of Satan's host bust open, squished to muck. The serpent's
crushed beneath his heel. Be jubilant, my feet.

My soul's on guard. I'm girded. I've got
my armor on. Ten thousand foes! I know the drill:
watch and fast and fight, wrestle and fight and pray.

And his tongue's a sword, did you know that? If
he sticks it out, he spears the foe nyah nyah
take that you bully. But the foe has hair

like arrows. Shakes his head and szzt they fly.
My man Jesus licks them right out of the air.
How cool is that? And his eyes are flame

blasting that prince of darkness. Though he with giants fight
he raises just one fist to squeeze them small, his knuckles
burnished rows of steel. His blood-red banner

streams afar, blood-rain falling into bloody seas, blood rising
high as a horse's bridle. End times. The last dread hour.
Fling open wide the golden gates and let the victors in.

Yeah, I want to meet the Lord in the air. I want
to smite the nations, the abominations. When the roll
is called up yonder, you bet I'll be marching as to war.

3. Mother

"Washed in the blood"

All day on my knees. I'm not complaining.
I was brought up to it: Eve's penitence,
Eve's penance. Labor is my sure defense
against the devil's lures. Idle hands: I
believe all that. If Eden's barred to me
for now, I'll work it off, that curse. I am

the handmaid. It's a careless world, always
dropping something, always scuffing it in
with heavy soles – muck off the streets, stray leaf,
fallen flower. What's impure requires
cleansing. I'm not complaining. On my knees
all day, I scrub it out, I scour it.

How did I come to marry? Old story.
I was brought up to it. He was wanting
what he wanted. Marry or burn. All day,
it seems like, on my knees: sometimes he wants
but can't. I work it hard. Labor is my
defense. I'm not complaining. He provides.

Spare the rod. I believe that too, raised them
by it, my kids. Scrubbed their mouths early so
they speak no evil. They're close-mouthed now. I'm
vigilant, track them by the hints they drop –
black threads unraveled, damp tissues shredded,
a pencil shaving. Why do the wicked prosper?

I mind the house. I mind him. Mind my tongue.
What else would I do? We know not the hour
when all must be cleansed. When I pray all day
on my knees, I'm not complaining. I am
the wise Martha, the faithful servant. If any
cup runneth over, I mop it spotless.

4. Father

"Working His purpose out"

This might come as a surprise. I'm no believer.
I take whatever comes. That's how I ended up
here: hard road, hot water, sea of troubles, quick sand.
Deadlines. The baby and the bank note falling due.

One punk kid, one mean tweener, the waddling wife –
all of them wild for Jesus. I go with the flow.
Easier that way. Keep my troubles to myself.
Accident and happenstance, and more on the way –

yeah, that's the kicker. This might be hard to credit
but here's what's floated me. Third day at the revival,
none of us sleeping, salt-sweated shirts, shouted hymns,
Bibles waved in the air, cried-out repentances,

pillars of cloud, shooting stars – when of a sudden
it was like a wind blew through me, like my eyes cleared,
like my tongue flamed, like all around me fell away,
and out of the whirlwind spake a still small voice, said

    Can't lose.

This might not be believed. I'm not a gambling man,
don't risk much, but who wouldn't bet on a sure thing?
Even after the tents come down and the preachers
roll off in their limos, I feel my election.

I'm been counting up the months until the Rising,
calculating out how much a day to keep them,
figuring the rent can go, the car can go, they
can eat until they don't need anymore to eat.

Deadlines. And if the date goes wrong again, can't lose.
If the house is emptied, if the door's left open,
who's to say it's not the Rapture? I ride the flow.
I take what's given. Keep my doubts to myself.

Crêche

At my godfather's house, the messenger
unlatched his case, lifted the lid, unswaddled
the perfect baby doll. Not cheap plastic, either,
but firm-fleshed, blushing. Then he uncoddled
the other small compartments: receiving
blankets, rompers, hand-knit booties, cute chapeaux.
If it were Barbie, you'd have said "trousseau."
I slunk outside, shoved hands in pockets, tried breathing.

How old was I? Too old for it, the raffle
too dear – and if they won it for my sister
all would be ruin: thorns in the flesh, hair
pulled and draggled. In my bed that night I
shut it out, though it kept knocking, baffled.
Worshipped in my own way, mean dog in the manger.

Strong Man

1. Campus

From the first hour we knew what he was,
a stone thrown hard and sharp into our waters. Kids
who'd swanned out collegiate not five minutes previous
shrank back cowed, deflated suddenly: banty or squab.
You could track him across campus by that emptiness,

that space around him. Other thugs might sneer,
might snicker, nudge each other, eyeing the chicks,
the cocks, beaking the barnyard. He
noticed no one, shared nothing. We were landscape
to him, poky as dirt or weed or scrub, his to walk over.

Have I said how attractive it was, the campus
crackling with menace, the air around him flaring?
Like girls at a party glamoured to be used – his one hand
over her mouth to keep her shut, his other
ramming her groin to keep her open – we

couldn't keep our eyes off him, equally stunned
and shunned, weeping and moistening, readied for him
almost without realizing. You never knew
what would come from his mouth when you called on him:
Lynching. Laughing. Tiny Tim should die. It was my job

to sharpen his logic, strengthen ever so socratically
his justifications: should die – why? So blame me
if you want for where he is now – except he never justifies,
sits smug in the emptied court, cushioned by air
he's sucked from the judges' lungs, every last lawyer

breathless as we were back then.

2. Who's This Philistine?

Who's this Philistine? For a ninety-pound stripling
raised up from the camps, sand flung in his face,
ash blown in his eyes, anyone that stand-up
would seem ten feet tall; anyone that armored
would seem brazen; anyone that rank would seem mighty
high and mighty. *Who's this uncircumcised Philistine?*
You can't help comparing. The staff of his spear
a weaver's beam. The heft of his coat expansive
with lashings of shekels of brass. Cocksure. Flagrant.

A kid who's that decided needs no persuading.
Am I a dog? When you've ranged where he's ranged,
scrapped where he's scrapped, you know a jackal
by its rendings, know a raptor by your hackles,
know an infidel for an infidel. *Am I a dog
that you come at me with staves?* Grown stringent
and stringy as a goat, he'll catch the lion by its beard
to shame his brothers; he'll champion the king
to shame the king; he'll cast the first stone.

What is my sin? The enemy flung
as from the center of the sling. *What
is my sin?* A pillow of goat's hair
for a bolster. *What sin?* No dowry
but a hundred foreskins. *Sin?* No more
than a dead dog, no more than a flea.
*Thrust me through, lest these uncircumcised
thrust me through and abuse me.* Lurking
among the lurking places. Five stones in a bag.

Hounded by Philistines (*am I a dog?*),
the hero slings whatever comes to hand –
brickbat, ashcan, landmine, bombshell,
quarrel, dudgeon, flak. After the beheadings,
the shouldered rocket launchers; the enemy

thrust under hoods, under harrows, under axes
of iron; houses thrown down brick on brick. Now Saul's
pinned to the wall, now Bathsheba's in the bath,
tell me, who once were ruddy, comely, much beloved

and cunning, who's the strong man now?

3. Thick

"A thick man," writes Bluto, eyeing self-satisfied
his girth in the pier glass – "a thick man's steady
in the storm, anchors fast as, um, an anchor, sails
full-bellied as a sail." That's it, he thinks: irrefutable,
the logic of tautology, she'll go for that.

"A thick man," he writes on, flexing his pectorals
so the medals wink and clink across his chest, so
his top buttons plip-pop – "a thick man's like a brick
in a foundation." No: too shaky for a town
of stone and steel: "like a brick in a brick wall." No:
too tame, too stolid, sedentary: "like a brick
chucked through a window" – just so: that dynamism.

"A thick man," he continues, spiking out absent-minded
his barbarosity of beard – "a thick man's cuddly
as a plumped and yallered Easter chick; reliable
as an old-time vaudeville schtick; slippery
and insidious as an oil slick; engrossing
as a splatter flick; efficient as a swift kick."
That's telling her. Now for romance: "a thick man's
slow as a cow's slow tongue at the salt lick."
Who could resist? He strokes his chin, considers,

and thinking of his enemy, how he twists all
to his unfair advantage, *beats me up
for doin' nothin'*, Bluto darkens,
glowers, thunders, storms: "a thick man
is not a sick man. A thick man is no hick."

And whaling out his arms so his brawn behemoths,
he lays the pen aside, bares broad his broad-toothed smile.
That's it, that's done it: just the thing to satisfy
a certain *heh-heh* GOYL, just the thing to justify
impounding a certain *heh-heh* OYL, just the thing
to put paid permanenk-like to any pipe-smacking
stubble-faced tattied Yankee runt whose only strength
is green-backs eaten shredded from a can.

4. How

> – *after P.W. Singer,* Children at War

How, when the mother prizes from her wrist the fingers,
grims yet more harsh her already grimaced face,
squints thee towards the roadway where already small gather
smaller in half-light set trudging, roads crowding crushed,
smallest twisted in small knots and fallen, knees sucked in
and thumbs sucked, backs walled up and bellies emptied, safe there
maybe dusk to dusk, maybe doss to doss, maybe dust to dust – ?

And how, when anyhow they come, unlooked for by day –
hen split, kid spitted scrawny – and some behind structures
they herd, where the guns barking, and in thy hands the stick
they stick, dust clotting red, and some with the machete
dis-armed – like logs, like kindling – and they say *stick*, and squint thee
towards the mother, her eyes grimmed shut, but whether to spurn
> or spare – ?

And how, though he has not sassed nor even whimpered,
when they squint out the brother for the lashing, and thou,
having known him longest, art to strike first, the sister
held down in the dust for the sticking, and he cries thee why,
what choice what other choice, the knuckles cracking – ?

And how, when they carve in thy flesh their sign,
binding the arms so not to soothe or smooth the fester,
and baptize thee, though thou weepest, in blood, though thou vomit,
naming thee now with thy blood name, not Paul but Saul, not David
> but Goliath – ?

So they say *knife*, you stab. So they say *stick*, you fall.
You now the stone that breaks the skull, though cast aside.
You now the mine that bites through bone, though left for dead.

So how best be strong, eh?
How be man?

IV

Still

> *Six months after Tura Satana's death, Gary Nakamoto photographs the audience in an extended exposure during a patio screening of Russ Meyer's* Faster Pussycat! Kill! Kill! *at Pizza Aiolo on Telegraph Avenue in Berkeley, August 10, 2011*

1.
There's a trick to these long exposures. You can't move
if you want to be seen. My friend tells me this, not
Gary. Gary's at the wheel, Gary's surfing the lanes,
Gary's somewhere out deep. My friend's gone along
for a lot of these shoots. Here's what he does: settles
himself for the length of the shot, which is to say
the length of the film. You'd think, my friend says, we're all
passive watchers, caught up by the screen, but no –
we all blur. Even the lovers rapt in the back row
move constantly their faces over each other, nudge aside
the collar, glide the hand through the hair. Even the boys
slouched low in the front row move constantly their hands
to their mouths, move constantly their feet. Even my friend
forgets himself, gets caught up in the action, laughs, startles,
shakes his head. My friend tells me this, not Gary. Gary
keeps his tricks to himself.

2.
We're early at Pizza Aiolo, so Gary
can set up the shoot, but nothing happens
while everything happens, every single thing
contingent on every other thing: before
the camera's positioned, the projector
must be positioned; before the projector
the nettle pizza, the corn-studded polenta;
before these main courses, the heirloom tomatoes,
the salmon, the salads, the pungent aioli; and
before that the cocktails, the spritzers,
the scuttling waitresses. As Tura Satana
will soon sneer on screen, *you can time that heap
with an hourglass*. Time yawns and stretches.
Gary waits it out.

3.
Gary's hunkered down at the patio's edge
watching the test pattern, figuring angles.
He's got to see what the camera will see: not
only our feet, not only the moon's slow streak
down the sky. We'll be watching the film, all eyes
and teeth and glitter. We're what the film would watch
if it weren't wound up in itself, if the film
had eyes. It can't see us licked by its flicker,
can't see us struck by its lights and darks. Gary
sees for it.

4.
8:13, and it's still not twilight, pink roses
splashed at the roofline, pink tablecloths and blue ones
splashed over with raucous flowers, yellow, red, red-orange.

8:24, and the plates, emptied, show leaf-green,
show sandy yellow, or is it sandy brown? people
leaning in, one to another, small candles.

8:31, and the grill's shut down, the far wall's
in shadow, people finding seats who were standing,
frat boys, bachelorettes, a woman bent over her cane.

8:37, and the standing burners flare
their copper warmth, the candles wink, bachelorettes
flash their candids, some city smolders out beyond us.

8:39, and it's too dark to see faces,
people carrying things pass in front of the screen,
pass in front of the lens, darkness carrying darkness.

5.
Gary's sitting at our table, between me and the film. I'm
watching the film, so I'm watching Gary. He's sitting in profile
like he's not watching, like he's not watching everything at once.
On screen, a strip club in riot. *Go baby go.* Gary looks
at the screen, looks at his watch. On screen, a woman in water,
breasts floating the surface. A car race. Strong eyebrows. Little gloves.
Gary eats, looks over his shoulder. *I don't beat clocks, just
people.* Wrestling in the sand. She strikes his neck. She breaks his spine.
Gary looks up: cloud cover. *Like a velvet glove cast in iron.*
On screen, something about Green Stamps: *2094 books
and I'll own the station.* Gary doesn't sit still, though he moves
in tight orbits. The moon's rising, occluded, almost oval,
so it looks to be hung crooked. *Sometimes I see her try
to figure me. I can't even figure myself. More stallion
than mare.* Gary bestirs himself. *Huff and puff and belch your smoke
and kill, and maim.* Waiters hover, stoop, reach. On screen, *what you eat
seems to settle in the right places.* Laughter, not all at once.
I can turn myself on a dozen different ways. Gary leans
back in his chair, looks over at Judy. Small smiles. *Do people
look different to you if they're not horizontal?* Next table,
clinking of glasses, light under faces. On screen, muscle guy
pushes a car away. Gary pushes forward, favors his back.
A couple runs straight along a railroad track. *I killed her like
she was an animal.* Gary looks up: overcast sky. Moon
falls behind buildings. Remember what Tura Satana said
early on to the guy who wants to see America first?
You won't find it down there, Columbus. Gary, in profile.

6.
In everybody's favorite scene, Varla –
that's Tura Satana – tries to crush a guy
against a wall, crush him with her car, but
he's strong as an ox, and he pushes back.
In Roger Ebert's phrase, *Meyer intercuts
his bulging muscles, holding back the car,
with her high-heeled foot, pushing down
the accelerator, and the tires
digging into the dust.* In real life, that
was Meyer's own car. He didn't want it hurt –
the tires wasted, the drive burnt out – and
figured the arm and the foot were enough
to get across the clash of wills. Satana
thought not. Found a shovel, dug a hole out,
threw in some loose dirt, put blocks underneath
so the tire could spin, stir it up, spit it out.
He's stuck and she's stuck, each trapped
in the straining. The tire's a blur.

7.
By the time she was seven, Tura Satana – born Yamaguchi –
had lived in two countries, been interned in one.

By the time she was ten, she'd been raped by a gang
of neighborhood toughs. Her father, to save her,
taught her karate. She tracked down those five men,
showed them what she could do, showed them who she'd become.

By the time she was fourteen, she'd formed her own gang –
"girls who kick butt." Juvie. Reform school. Her parents,
to save her, married her off to a family friend
down the Mississippi, himself seventeen, but

by fifteen she was burlesquing, out on her own –
martial arts and tassel twirling. Harold Lloyd
photographed her erotically, praised to her face
her symmetrical face, told her "you should be seen."

By nineteen or twenty she found herself pregnant,
danced on for eight months. She's raised two daughters.
By twenty-five or so – I'm not making this up –
she'd dated Elvis Presley, dated Frank Sinatra,
was acting for TV, and in *Irma la Douce*.

She was twenty-seven when Russ Meyer cast her.
"I took a lot of my anger," she told one interviewer,
"and I let it loose." Meyer said – it was a compliment –
"Don't fuck with her.... She might turn on you."

By the time she was thirty, Ted Mikels, in a club, witnessed
a woman throw at her "this humongous ashtray,
this lead-crystal ashtray," and – as she tells it –
"in five steps I had her up against the wall, because
I was so livid." Mikels later told her, "I had to come home
and write the movie for you.... The look on your face
was enough to scare anybody." That was *Astro-Zombies*.

By her mid-thirties, she'd been shot in the gut
and starred in three films. Then she left show-biz.

Nurse. Police radio operator.
Dental receptionist. By forty-two, she'd married
an ex-cop. Good years. Then a car accident,
her back broken, two years spent in surgeries
but she didn't stop. Hotel security. Comics conventions.

When I watched Pussycat, I knew nothing about her,
figured she died shrunken, that Hollywood cliché.
Harold Lloyd was right. She should be seen.

8.
In Gary's finished print, the structures stand still:
buildings, roses, burners, tables, benches.
The people seem vague. Two rows in the back,
faceless and faded, family portraits
from some other century. Then smudges,
impressions, too far and too fast. Then there's
three tables, three whirlwinds, subtle flashes
of flesh, a napkin, a bottle, a purse.
Gary's in front. His white shirt and khakis
soak up the light, and the way that he's moved –
now forward, now back – has doubled his heft.

I want to be seen. I've tried not to move.
In the finished print, I can see my face
between Gary's back leaning forward and
Gary's chest leaning back. It's like the mask
of Agamemnon settled on his shoulder.
Closer in, someone's left two wineglasses
sitting out on a bench, a white sweater
on the ground behind them. The way light strikes
off their globes and lips and concavities,
it's like time's breaking open over there
without any of us noticing.

V

Fresh Air

To move again inside one's clothes
And every garment a caress –
Arm sleeved in air, and the collar open.

To move again. Butterfly effects.
Lavender rising in crisp waves
Where air's a promise, wings in the wind.

Cloud against cloud, the faintest scrape.
The cloth falls seamless now as water.
Silk shirt. Linen cloud. Lithe sheets of rain.

Around the bed, it's hunt and gather.
The hunger comes. The hunger goes.
The mulberry half hidden. The sheet's loose whisper.

To move again, and all a billow.
Swing and lift. Trade thick for thin.
And the splash at the ankle, up and out.

Feathers preened sleek to a ruffled neck.
Cyclones glimpsed at the eye's far reach.
The shirt tail flap. Air slapping back.

Winter's gone. Slow wing of hair.
Soft sparks struck where the inseam chafed.
Maybe a nostalgia, but move again.

Inked

With two days' rain, the mulberry
turns insipid, a purple blurt,
a swashy splurge of nothing. But
an hour of sun restores to it
its toothiness, its woodiness,
its subtle after-savor, like
a perfumed person just walked by,
and a brisk night will brace it back
to tartness. It seems a long wait
while green nubs bobble out pink flesh,
bruise red, red violet, blue black,
black, but once the turning starts, they'll
keep on turning: browse it down when
you leave the house, and thirty more
will ready by the time you're back
from marketing. Let birds wheel out
above you, squabbling for fruit
through the upper branches. What they
can't see is tucked up under leaf,
each branch glistering, limbs arched out
like the eaves of an umbrella,
a secret cave of jewels. Say
the devil blacks his boots with them;
say Pliny called them the wise fruit:
both make it the poet's tree. You
shelter there while the storm comes on,
your fingers inked, and your tongue
inkier, gobbling fast before
the rain can wash them out again.

Omens

So strange I'll state it baldly: two embryos turn up
on the porch one morning, each to its own flowerpot,
sheltering there under the Thai, the lemon basil,
nakedly pink, the size of a fat thumb, each wriggling
in its skin. I can see they're intending to be birds,
can guess they've fallen featherless from great heights – though (strange)
no tree shades us here, nor any scrap of nest or shell
fell with them. Their limbs move; their mouths gape; they bulge
with dark, broken but still possible, a test I'll never pass.

Just days later, when the boy comes mowing, another,
this one with a tail. It's pink and pig-like, nosing blind
into the high grass where the mower slashes, wriggling
in its skin. I can guess it's intending to be squirrel,
can see it's fallen hairless from great heights, though it's shed
its origins with its future: no shreds of nest or
broken branch rest with it. How large must they fall before
I take the meaning? The world goes on
aborting itself while – obscurely responsible,
ineptly irresponsible – I shovel it up,
lay it down in the bushes for the neighborhood fat cats.

Lawn Boys

I swear it's the mayhem that gets them going,
revving those little motors without the first
shred of a permit. This latest one runs through
two gas cans easy, just tanking around, rearing
the housing up on its hind wheels, toeing its nose
smack down into the borders, throttling, choking –
yes, a carte blanche invitation to destroy.

Whatever gets them off the couch, it's not the lawn
itself. These guys aren't gardeners, can't read the line
dividing sod from shrub, grassplot from seedbed.
They'll put the parrot-tulips to the blade, slice
right through violets and fern brakes, yet leave untouched
a pride of thistles, a bristle of dandelions –
"so pretty." And nor is it the money, else

they'd be here more often. First of spring, I call
and call, while the grass thickens to pasture, then
to wildwood, then to spinney. This latest one
has set his phone to seem he's answered: "Wait a sec!
My battery's low! I'll just grab the extension – "
then a long pause, then some well-recorded fumbling, then
more mutters just before the razzy beep. I leave him

long detailed messages I know he won't play through.
That's why – must be – that rise by the front walk's
razed raw again, why the side-yard's gone to briars.
"Take care," I'll tell the phone; "there's deadwood fallen,"
but that won't slow him: he won't pick up sticks, grinds through
whatever's in his way, shredding plastic bags and paper,
shattering branches – once even a brick

to see its splinters scatter and fly. My daddy mowed
sedately, sober as a farmer guiding the plow
behind the plodding mule, methodical,
meticulous. These guys are rough-riders,

lathering their broncs up San Juan Hill, and I
must like that better. Mayhem. What else
do I get? What else do I pay them for?

Reunion

On the very afternoon when the mimosas shifted,
folding in their feathery fans to swag their sleeves in coin,
who should turn up again but Ulysses, fleshier himself
these days, and similarly dripping with gold. Came back

tale-telling, gregarious, as full of himself as ever,
the face, the body thickened with experience but still
approximating unmistakably the man she'd known,
the ring big on his finger, the eyes holding hers. Came back

apologizing for the past however many years when
(always the wily one, always after something) he'd used her
ill, he said. Then back to his tale of mayhem, all of it
certainly diverting – though, from what did he divert her?

On the very afternoon when the cicadas stilled themselves
for whole unsettling minutes while the winds changed their courses,
she stood there similarly stunned, caught strangely wrong-footed,
not sure what she should be feeling. How had her story

turned into one of his, the nostalgia so thick on the air
he was near to weeping with it? An invitation
that wouldn't be an invitation. (You didn't think I
meant Penelope? Swine and swineherd, pigsty and pig.) Like

in all those years she hadn't again and again moved on,
thinking of him, sure, from time to time, but nevertheless
disconcerted to find she'd loomed so large and long and lush
in his imagination. What was it he was wanting?

Hard to say. War had made him more strategic. And what
might she make him, make of him? If they first met today, would even
their bodies speak? She thought so, maybe, way past flirtation,
drowned out by the cicadas, among the crass mimosas.

Practicing Old

In the ice of the Ice Moon, dark
of the Dark Moon, how slick
the sole slops in its shoe, how sharp
the ankle angles. See that stiff branch,
all quirk and excrescence? Imagine it

fallen. Twigs in a heap. Leaves raked
skeletal. And the voice cracked too –
all shin and clavicle, the rib unhinged, hip
unsocketed, a scraped voice, scuffed voice,
skinned, and the Blood Moon blown bony,

landing hard on the heel of the hand.
In the storm of the Storm Moon, wind
of the Wind Moon, so simple
to sallow, let the lips sere
to willow, rub the lashes

spare, cough out the tongue. Who lives
like this? No one you know. Yet the fog
frays you, wind blows you down. Managed once
in the Blue Moon, twice the next, thrice
the one following – see now with what

accomplishment you stagger
on the stair. Is this the harvest
of the Harvest Moon? Not quite
second nature yet, but
getting there, getting there.

Poll

Borough Hall, Rutledge, Pennsylvania
November 2, 2010

1.
They blow through in gusts, strong-armed in
by the raw day, coat collars up
and the hands chafing, smacked straight past
the eddy of politicos
blustery in the side-room, those straws
in the squall. Children dragged in blue-faced,
blue-knuckled, learning democracy,
and the elders with their backs up
scudding along the cold winds of change.

2.
Dirty weather. Out of the storm,
stalwarts circle the side-room, itching
to buttonhole. From coffee pot
to doughnut box, they drift, snag, ebb.
Hauled inside by a handshake truce
and – while they're in – forbidden their
electioneering, they're nearly
silted up, their silent surge and
seethe and spate rippling into
shoals and shallows, volatile oil
in the waters. One stamps his feet,
mudslinging. One lurks, umbrella
drubbed against pants-leg. One hedges,
skirts. One stands for hours, jawing,
fists open-and-closing. Call it
a wash-out, for all that undertow, though
each still secretly hopes for groundswell.

3.
At the booth, the watcher draws back
the curtain to a tiny stage, bows
the actor on, drops the cloth. Each Punch
or Judy stands to the same mark,
stands firm, stands fagged, stands fidgety –
that leg-show: work-boot to loafer,
sweats to jeans to cords to pinstripes,
down at the heels, up on the toes,
hobble skirt to hoop skirt, every
sort of legging. By day's end, it's
a fog, a haze, a scrim, a blurred
run-through: a people's mind or stance
constantly steadily changing.

Concourse

"He ran," she says, "ran the whole way, and me
in the wheelchair." Who's she telling? Her voice
carries, so it's hard to say which of us
might talk back if she paused a sec: we've all
been running, but the wheelchair trumps us. "Ran,"
she says, "right up to the gate, and can't see
no plane. Thought they'd left," she says, "without us."
The van's silent. We've all been left like that,
left flightless. "Five airports today," she says,
"five carriers, pop prop out of Denver
and still can't get to Philly." No one can.
The van shakes, packed tense with the ten of us,
shimmies as it corners. We've hop-scotched, too,
airport to airport; jumped through loop-de-loops
to get here; we've pitched, dragged, and whip-stalled; but
not in a wheelchair. "Used to be," she says,
"I'd ride behind him on the Harley." He
has the jacket, has the grizzle – we all
marked him back at baggage. He rides silent
up there by the driver, his bristles and
his shavings picked out in the headlights: shot-
gun, pistol. "Now," she says, "he pushes me
ahead. Wherever we go," she says, "I
get there first." In the snowy dark, he smoothes
his moustache. Might or might not be smiling.

Cold Hands

Midwinter's not the best time for remembering you're a female,
Socks thickening your ankles three-fold up and down the snowy driveway.
You used to swing those hips. Now you can't find them.
Coat over coat over coat over cardigan.

The girls flirt by along the sidewalk you've just shoveled,
Jackets flapped back from rosy busts, from bellies bold as Barbados.
Even their boots show trim and dainty, skipping the icy patches.
Their laughter lifts their filmy scarves fluttery as flamingo.

Out here, when you're blushing, cold tweaks your nose red, pinches till it runs.
Where the hoop slides through your earlobe, the hole's iced over.
Used to be hot-rods, fast cars, boys quick to get the top off.
Now it's eiderdown, it's wadded silk, it's cotton batting.

All the lush and luscious ceremony of bedding?
Quilt over quilt, wool over flannel.
Jump in under fast with your five layers of clothes on. You want
Hands mittening your hands. You want to keep your socks on.

Roots

Aunt Nell surprised even herself
with that rinse tint. Fed to the teeth
with the loose and dingy droops, she
wanted froth, she wanted airy.
Like Miz Belzer, snow-swept, regal.
Like Miz Heyward, cloud-capped and cute.
But first time out, the rinse wronged her,
sallowed, soured: too tentative
a blonding. The sun rising on
twigs shriveled by winter: no leaf
or bloom but maybe a turning:
a baby's furze, a tallow veil,
a jaundice. She'll blush to the roots,
the grizzled roots, but it's not spring.

Veiling

The last of winter's hazing: a high gale
whacking through the branches, the brittle twigs
scritching each other, the chaff sent flying.
It's grey up there, stick against stick, each limb
striking out blindly; fingers lost, and thumbs;
knuckles scuffed, elbows skint, arms abraded.

It's no wonder there's a fever starting,
a little flush, a swelling at the joints.
The tip of each twig's cocked now to bursting
and, stick against stick, rubs itself rosy.
Look up: like a cloud left hanging over night
the grey's blushing, dawning soft, a mauve air.

And then the flocking. Leaf on leaf stitched in
and overstitched, so hastily the thread's
left dangling, stem stitch over laid stitch
over couching; wheat stitch on feather stitch
on thorn; crow's foot over fly stitch on spider's web.
French knot. Chinese knot. Whipped satin.

Thus the sheerest tulle layers into veiling,
the palest fern mantilla muffles into
mossy chenille. What was winter up to,
that seemed so raw, so cruel? It's all grown
hazy, leaves cowling out, clouding over
the hard hardwood, shrouding the skeleton.

Catch

Stranded on the corner where they're airing out the air.
That's what she's been dreaming. Some strain of it, strand of it
stroking her lip. Some little cat's paw, some soft clawing.

Breath with a catch in it. Catch in the throat. A breath that's
almost catchy. Might one follow its drift? tug its tail?
wind it like the wind around a finger?

And if I cough it up – some thick dreadlock of snarled hair,
some kestrel's casting, some owl's indigestible – ?
To catch at straws. That's what she's been dreaming.

Air striped and roughened in the breathing of it, air
like a roughening tongue. And where it falls, a subtlety:
a pleasantness, a pleasantry. Or else a purring?

Clouds running. Long arms of wisteria reaching and
bobbing and rising. Everything rustling. A freshness
on the upper lip. A slip along the upper arm. Yet

no more than a lightening, a loosening, a lessening.
Stranded on the island where three dreams meet.
Underneath the evergreens the freshest air.

Quite the catch. Didn't quite catch. My fae
more svelte than your fae. My fair folk the more fair.
The flick at the tip of the wind's tail.

That's what she's been dreaming.

VI

Dead Doll

1.
Too thin skinned always, the sort
best kept to a shelf, yet always
he was skying, he was always
avalanching himself. So first

as if frost bit, of the one hand gone
the fingers; then, fist first, the other
as if frost-beaten, ice-shivered,
the whole arm from the arm-hole gone

as if wholly eaten; and the left foot
crushed off; of the foot left uncrushed
the Achilles heel gone flimsy; and
on the last limb a piercing –

curved elegance, a Bodhi-leaf
whimsy curled to the arm and
tattooed through, a piercing third-eye
gaze into nothing – but otherwise

unchanged for nearly sixty years,
that baby face not aging a day, lips
pinked and pursed, cheeks and chin plumped in
full as his sister's, and the same rolled hair.

2.
Well, that's all done. This last fall's
cold-cocked him, knocked him cock-eyed, crack-
pated. His jaunty hat's turned skull-cap, blows
and bowls about, pawn for every cat's paw. Clothes

make the man, they say – and unmake:
his sister bends at the hip, sits tight beneath her dirndl
wherever you leave her. Stuck from the start
in stiff lederhosen, he could always ever only

stand and fall, stand and fall. One of a passel
smuggled post-war through the checkpoints
by my kindly Aunt Corinne: plumed aristo,
oak-foot Dutch girl, tammed and wild-haired Scot –

all of them shock-eyed, all of them shaky, all of them
standing nevertheless their new ground, and him
the lone rover. Now for sure he's Euro-trash: crack-up,
casualty, cavity, chasm. That's what jaunty gets you.

3.
Were I Isis, I'd be picking up the pieces, lifting
his face, backing that jigsaw with muslin,
getting precise with tweezer and glue-stick. But no,
I'm not that girl. Stay put, don't go anywhere,

I tell his sister: these sixty-some-odd years I've
been bossing her around. She doesn't move a muscle,
doesn't turn a hair – but lately, when I glance her way,
she's standing, balanced, digging in the baby-doll toes

you can see through the boot black, the child
she still is shaping her face to her brother's, pursing
the baby-doll lips as though wondering where
he's gone. I think she's thinking she's been good too long.

Show Runner

Scheherazade's working these days in L.A.,
splitting her time between studios, between
film and TV. Those story arcs that leave us
one raised foot from the cliff's edge, from the troll's ax,
from the sweet kiss – that's all on her; and bullets
that strike our man down (disaster!) on one night
to bounce, the next week, off his bullet-proofing –
that's her signature move. Upshot. Double-take.
Bluff tending towards lure, epilogue towards sequel.

But don't you marvel at how she keeps us hooked,
keeps us up watching half the night? Stale re-runs,
even, have me binging. My favorites? Movies
that repeat themselves, chase their own tails, unroll
their own remakes: *Groundhog Day, Fifty First Dates,
Run Lola, Memento, Godot*. It's like she
knows this is something we can't hear just the once
and profit by it. Like she knows we can't rest
until we know how things pan out tomorrow

and tomorrow, and tomorrow. Think of all
she does, whirling like a dervish plot to plot,
granting wishes like a djinn – which is to say
ambiguously, promising always tales
even stranger and more wonderful, pauses
as delicious as her words, whispering *what
I shall tell*, up past dawn with her sweet nothings.
So much recorded in my DVR, I could be
watching already for a thousand and one nights.

Mystery

I'd got to page one-eighty-five, eighty-six
of the latest nail-biter crime novel, when
she made me gasp, my spunky smart-mouthed scapegrace
heroine-sleuth: shadowing her mark, she'd stalked
down those mean streets, straight through the sleazy bar-lounge
of the flea-bag hotel, out its dim back hall
past the ladies' to the men's room, yes right in
and up to the urinal where the bad guy

pissed, was pissed, was pissant, pissing. *That's ballsy*,
I thought, seriously impressed, while she sneered
something strong-armed and snarky, something screwball
and scampish, scathing, scofflaw, then really proved
she had 'em: unzipped, pissed on his shoes, re-zipped.
How'd she manage that? I actually asked,
before I saw what any other reader
knew from page one: Leslie – *call me Les* – was male.

I had to re-think it all: how she'd stepped up
for her pal in that bar fight; how she'd faced down
shysters and cops; how at the pick-up game she'd
razzed the young toughs; how she'd tossed back a few; how
she'd sat the edge of the secretary's desk,
leaning in, almost leering; how her forehead
rested a beat against her own front door; how
she ducked her mom's calls. Everything audacious

drained of its color: male, merely male, merely
conventional, a dick like any other.
This happens to me all the time. Doctor Jay,
Architect Nance, Chef Zee: I anticipate
women. Surgeon. Game warden. Airline pilot.
Sanitation worker. Boxer. Professor.
You name the job; I see a woman there. So
for you, guys, does it happen the other way? When

Jay pulls the pizza from the oven; when Nance
sets the last dish in the rack; when Zee sighs deep,
shifting her weight in the empty bed; when Chris,
though coughing, turns the page; when Dani beckons,
soothes; when Tam tears up, smiles anyhow; when
Gianni hunches her shoulders; when Audie sings;
when Billie whistles; when Les puts her hard hand
to her mouth, thinking twice, do you see that man?

Celebrity

Myself, in Japan

Every day the interviews, the flash-POP-pop
of the paparazzi, waves of waves, shout-outs
from strangers; and each time as disconcerting
as the first: through placid pedestrians, twelve
twelve-year-olds in blue school uniforms squealing
and rushing, rushing at her, rushing her. She
thought first they'd just grabbed some random bystander
to snap them, and she the most random – happy

of course to oblige – but no: what they wanted
was twelve photographs, each one with her in it
and in it with them: proof she existed, proof
they existed together. It must have been
field-trip season: kids lining up for buses
everywhere, or scavenging for souvenirs,
and she the latest thing, the latest prize. *Don't
let it go to your head*, she'd razz herself, but

it was heady. In twos and threes they'd stalk her,
or they'd crowd in, whole classes of them, hefting
their questions, raising their fingers in little
rabbit-eared Vs, not meaning victory, not
meaning peace, and not what cockney louts intend
with their rude two fingers, but evidently
only *Cheezits! Take me now!*, a semaphore
to the photographers. She thought of shaking

the hand once of the Secretary of State –
of course no true connection, and yet the zing,
the anxious exhilaration, the ozone
of power. Or glimpsing at the stage door once
the actor with whom later in the theatre
she'd shared the same stale air: how ordinary
in his ordinary clothes, and yet the thrill
of his proximity. What's celebrity

but the commonplace made stranger, the stranger
commodified? She knew her true face value
but saw too how her swelled head signified, how
through fair trade she inflated. So when kids pressed
at Hiroshima for her opinions, for her least words, she
set aside her guilt and sorrow, answered each shy hi
with *hai*, smiled for each camera, gave back what she
owed for being someone, anyone, in the world.

Glass Beach

1.
Imagining Glass Beach, she saw the sea
scrub down the sky, the sky sluice off the sea,
and both so see-through the gulls couldn't help
crashing into first one then the other.

Saw the silicates accumulate, a sift
of sugar, a sprinkling of salt,
and all so delicate, the wet-footed
walked on glass, sandaled in finest foam.

2.
Imagining Glass Beach, where the drunks
bash their bottles, smashed wine-dark, smashed pea-green –
thick lips, hollow necks, coins rolled out of pockets,
waves breaking their broken ribs edgier and smaller.

Where – pummeled and pumiced – there's no more razor's edge,
there's no more splintering. Sea glass. Shards of starlight.
Shivers of permafrost. Snatches of rippling sea.
Shell pink. Pearl grey. All dawn's soft scintillations.

3.
Imagining Glass Beach, reaching for crimson
among sea-frosted pebbles, but ugh: thumb sunk
in spongy glut, in gizzards of give. Polymers
unraveling. Bags spattered, tattered into opacity. Styrofoam.

Reaching and retching she could clean all this,
this sludge and tar, this gob and glob, this shard and shred –
trash to bag, bag to dump, dump to fill, fill to scow.
Horse Latitudes. Everything circling. Pacific Drift. Sargasso Sea.

4.
Imagining the glass coffin where everyone sees
her molder, sees the hair surge and swirl, the nails
claw out. Or imagining the glass hill where every comer
slips and slides, horses all in a foam – and she at the top, responsible.

Who'd blame Cinderella for the chipped toe,
the cracked heel, the crazed vamp, the soiled sole
of the glassy slipper slipped off on the stairs? The one sister's bunions.
The one sister's blisters. Who'd blame Cinderella? Dirty beast that you are.

5.
Imagining Glass Beach, she remembers
the Philadelphia Water Works, where for ninety years
the Schuylkill powered the pumps that lifted the Schuylkill,
where pipes of spruce and yellow pine sluiced it around.

If beauty is use, what's natural? Today
at the Water Works Museum, a glass case shows
what washes up and what silts down. The glitter of all
she's broken. The scum of her shampoo. Long strands of her hair.

Englands of the Mind

Prim prams, and all the hedges hollied,
the trim leaves prickly – back-bent, spine-sprung,
congregations of sharp archings. And
ankleted in bells – blue bells, Morris
harnessings, long falling steeple peals,
a starchy jangle. The baby's rattle.

And every book a wild wood, letters
vine-twined, brambled; each sentence choke-chocked,
thrusting its leaves out; the very oaks
of thought wrenched up, wrung tight in galls, burls,
gnarls, knots, kinks, cankers, gaping hollows,
pinching fingers. Children lost in there.

And every border over-planted,
leaf shoved against leaf, blossom lording
over blossom, stems louting out to
elf-lock, rat-tail, haw. Whose hooligans?
I wanted in, wanted the rooms, too –
gadrooned, wainscoted; black oak panels

hewn to intricacy, splintered, flayed,
pitch-blackened. Even the coziest
thatched cottage: something enigmatic
in the kitchen, something hermetic
at the priest hole, something occulted
on the downs. Every austerity

sacramental. Whiskered knights pounding
a round table. Belts maiden-braided
of maiden's hair. Boys laughing up their
embroidered sleeves. Girls finding themselves
in laidly worms. I could be like that,
be bold, be bold: ice-edged, steel-etched.

Autumn, Casa Batlló

> *... the eye of a whirlwind ...*
> – Casa Batlló, Juan José Lahuerta, tr. Steve Cedar

Oak curdled to caramel
and plaster swirled in a silky batter –
      piece of cake
kept long in the cupboard
skim crackling off the milk
the butter gone rancid

Water shatters in the sink
      shatters the sink

She's bedded down in dry rot and wood worm
motes rising and falling
      the blue note and the yellow
and the undulated jamb splitting artistically
      waves, wrinkles, folds
      great drops held in suspension

Air shatters against the glass
      shatters the glass

Senyora, your bones are showing

And when did the black lace, hoarded,
fray to tatters in its drawer?
Or the great-grandmother's heirloom shawl,
its silk fringe fly-away as hair?

Fire shatters around the hearth
      shatters the hearth

And the walls
lit as if from within,
the parquet dimming

The shawl flung down over the piano

      (no space for a piano,
but were there a piano)

its moaré so frail, a chord shatters across it
      shatters it

Somebody's Saints March In

Surprises at the 1995 Eagle Wing Music Festival, Groomsport, County Down
For Tram Turner and Jim Doane

Not your expected Irish music: no sainted mother
pleading with the Virgin for her boy Danny's safe return;
no four fields sprouting up together, uniformly green;
no celestial Gaeltacht voices winging on their grace notes
into heaven; no bodhrán, no uilleann pipes, no whiskey-
driven risings at the wake. No: this here is Ulster music,
ballads gearing up to blue-grass, a sound demonstration
of trans-Atlantic pollination, and three friends from the South
are listening intently, dubious but open to persuasion, eager

to be even-handed. Three friends from the South on a lark
in the North, June of the first cease-fire, dark Belfast over
their shoulders, sunlight scattering in wavery fractals
on the wind-crisped water, just like back home; the music tinny,
thinned by the breeze, muffled in thick talk, dulled by the children's
squealing, blaring and dimming as the amplifiers surge
and fail, just like back home; sails on the bay, hot fish pungent
with vinegar, and three friends at their ease, basking in the warmth,
the Northern hospitality, cooled by the brisk air – June,

before things heat up again. Three friends from the South, and this
is who they are: Charleston, Chattanooga, Chapel Hill – seeds
cast on the waters, scattered maybe from this very port,
sprouting out bog cotton, indigo, blue grass: trans-Atlantic
pollination. Who they are: two men, one not; one in love,
two not; two embraced by doting families, one (alas) not;
one devout, two not; two gay, but all three in their own way queer;
one Irish-speaking, two not; two Irish-dancing, one – oh,
rather not; two raised in the deep South, one not; one settled

in the Southland, two not. Among them, such lilting music –
Chieftains, Altan, Solas. Among them, such stirring marches,
sit-ins, demonstrations – Civil Rights, Equal Rights, Gay Pride,
Anti-War, Anti-Nuke, Right to Choose, Take Back the Night. Which
is why, of all the festive people gathered here – families

lounging on rough blankets; men standing stoic in shirt-sleeves, arms
hugged tight to pale bodies; codgers sipping dark pints; toddlers
sitting down abruptly; teens in their blond dreads and piercings;
mothers relaxing at last, feet up, indulgent – these three

are the only ones to blink and gape when out of the dazzling sun
a grey mist rises and solidifies – ten men, twenty
in grey uniforms, stars in their eyes and on the crossed blue
bars of their snapping red battle flags, the band whistling
Dixie, the crowd hooting and hollering for their Lost Cause
as the Ulster Re-Enactors of the War Between Our States
march out to strut their stuff. Old times there are not forgotten.
The sun clouds over, the wind picks up, the soldiers shout. Which
South will rise? Three friends look away, look away, look away.

Berlin, Belfast, Belgrade, Baghdad, Basra

Too many wars. Jarred awake, the house broken,
the brute butt of a gun against the pretty
dish your neighbor brought you – look around, so much
to lose. The shoes you bought for style and thrift will
flay your feet on the rain-swept road; the photo
folded next to your heart will rip with your dress;
your scrubbed flesh will turn rancid; you will eat filth
and hope for more of it. Tell me you haven't
yet imagined this, felt the knife at your throat,
seen your own uncle's blood on the kitchen floor.

Too many wars. Safe in our sealed car, nations
away, we hear the blood splatter, trickling through
the radio's local concerns – three minutes,
maybe, every hour. Refugees, thousands,
spill over the borders, seep back in, a sponge
squeezed and loosened, loosened and squeezed. Returning
to devastation, they want their turn-about,
and who can blame them – the neighbors, however
many cakes they bring or glad embraces, did
not save them, can never look the same. Beyond

the signal's reach, we twist the dial: too many wars,
three minutes each, the wrongs festering, the blood
rancid, the neighbors hesitating too long
before knocking, cake and dish in hand – and who,
Lord, is my neighbor? Which of us drops the gun
first? Which takes or eats the cake? Which speaks sweet reason
so as not to change a thing? Unmarked ourselves
by knife or chilling blood today, no one we know
cowering in the roadside ditch as our car whips by,
we twist the dial as tourists do, just neighbors.

VII

Four Snow Moans

1.
Snow moon. Slow snow moon. Slow falling,
falling full, falling slow, already fallen through
to dawn. Slow blows of snow and
the sky winded, scrolled and winded.

    Bitte, bitter beauty.

Soft slaps, slow slaps, with the sting
of a ring to them. Slow wince in crystal.
Veiled moon, staggered – stars, diamonds –
slow-dragging the weighted veils.

2.
All day, intermittent, down the roof, a gravelling –
or no: a gravitation, a corrugation. Rocks gouged
out the throat, hawked off. Growlers calving.

    Speak, spectral avalanche.

Did you think it would go easy, sloughing it over?
A growl rasped to groaning. An eave left hanging.
Roof stripped to its pith. Gutter scraped to guttural.

3.
Rain over snow, blown low over snow,
low smoke of snow, that exhalation.

Wading the nimbus, who wouldn't be changed?
Snow-breath. White-out. A breathing in. A swallowing.

    Bide, shrouded bride.

A mist adrift among the drifts, a mist drifting.
Stilled stiff underfoot: the slick bite, the powdering chill.

See what comes of it? See what comes
open-mouthed to the long moaning?

4.

Snowmelt. The ground's a slobber. The sidewalk's mud-faced, frost-feathered. Street's flushed with it.

    Drink up, thirsty girl.

Every shrub slumped. Every blade bruised. But moss already greening: plush archipelagoes
        down the cracked driveway.

Zueignung

Eye bright. Sky bright. Glazed pavement.
Twigs whittled by wind, whistling
their sharp marks hard up there, black
honed against blue, dry-point flocked
with nibs, tracery fringing
the canopy's edge, gaze glanced
among glazings, the grass too
glass-edged, bladed, blazing, grit
glittering, random branches
branching random to somehow
predictable silhouettes,
all the world's thin bones shining.
Sky wash. Eye wash. New glasses.

What comes from last night's weeping,
all that walloping and wailing:
another gift she'll never know she gave me.

Notes

"The Librarian": "the snow keeps turning / and turning its white pages" echoes Denise Levertov's "To the Reader": "and as you read / the sea is turning its dark pages, / turning / its dark pages."

"Packed for the Afterlife": Titled after an article in *Archaeology*, March/April 2015, with details from various issues of the magazine.

"King of the Cats": "My friends, there are no friends" echoes Jacques Derrida in "Politics of Friendship," where he echoes Montaigne echoing Aristotle; or – for another source entirely – Coco Chanel. I thank Nora Johnson for alerting me to this resonant phrase.

"Rapture": In addition to Biblical sources, "Brother" draws on hymns by Henry Alford, St. Andrew of Crete (tr. John Mason Neale), Sabine Baring-Gould, John Bunyan, George Heath, Reginald Heber, William Walsham How, Julia Ward Howe, Martin Luther, Thomas Joseph Potter, Lawrence Tuttlett, Isaac Watts, and Charles Wesley. The line "Fling open wide the golden gates and let the victors in" comes from Henry Alford's "Ten Thousand Times Ten Thousand."

"Who's This Philistine?": For David and Goliath, see 1 Samuel, 17.
  – "Who's this uncircumcised Philistine?": David, 1 Samuel, 17: 26.
  – "Am I a dog...?": Goliath, 1 Samuel, 17:43.
  – "What is my sin?": David, 1 Samuel, 20:1. The details of stanza 3 are drawn from David's career of guerrilla warfare, as Saul seeks preemptively to kill him.
  – "Thrust me through...": Saul, 1 Samuel, 31:4.
  – "Under harrows of iron, and under axes of iron": 2 Samuel, 12:31.

"Thick": "Beats me up for doin' nothin'": from the Popeye cartoon "Assault and Battery."

"Show Runner": Italicized phrases excerpted from *The Arabian Nights*, translated by Husain Haddawy, based on the text of the fourteenth-century Syrian manuscript edited by Muhsin Mahdi, Norton 1990.

"*Zueignung*": "Dedication," a setting by Richard Strauss of a poem by Hermann von Gilm, with the refrain "*Habe Dank.*"

About the Author

Nathalie Anderson received the Washington Prize from The Word Works in 1998 for her first book, *Following Fred Astaire*, and her book *Stain* was selected by Eduardo C. Corral in 2017 for the Word Works' Hilary Tham Capital Collection. Other publications include *Crawlers*, *Quiver*, and the chapbook *Held and Firmly Bound*. Anderson collaborated in 2021 with artist Susan Hagen and poet Lisa Sewell on *Birds of North America*, and her poems have appeared in such journals as *Atlanta Review*, *DoubleTake*, *Natural Bridge*, *The New Yorker*, *Nimrod*, and *Plume*. She has also authored libretti for five operas, in collaboration with Philadelphia composer Thomas Whitman. Anderson recently retired from Swarthmore College, where she served as Alexander Griswold Cummins Professor of English Literature and directed the Creative Writing program.

About the Artist

Randall Exon received his MFA from University of Iowa and his BFA from Washburn University. His work can be found in the collections of the Pennsylvania Academy of Fine Arts, Philadelphia, PA; the Ballinglen Museum of Art, Ireland; and other private collections. His paintings have been featured in solo and group exhibitions across the country and at the Hirsch & Adler Modern Gallery in NY. He has received a number of awards and fellowships including a Henry Luce Fellowship to Indonesia in 1985. He is the Sarah Lawrence-Lightfoot Professor of Art at Swarthmore College where he has taught in the Department of Art and Art History since 1982.

About The Word Works

Since its founding in 1974, The Word Works has steadily published volumes of contemporary poetry and presented public programs. Its imprints include The Washington Prize, The Tenth Gate Prize, The Hilary Tham Capital Collection, and International Editions.

Monthly, The Word Works offers free programs in its Café Muse Literary Salon. Starting in 2023, the winners of the Jacklyn Potter Young Poets Competition will be presented in the June Café Muse program.

As a 501(c)3 organization, The Word Works has received awards from the National Endowment for the Arts, the National Endowment for the Humanities, the D.C. Commission on the Arts & Humanities, the Witter Bynner Foundation, Poets & Writers, The Writer's Center, Bell Atlantic, the David G. Taft Foundation, and others, including many generous private patrons.

An archive of artistic and administrative materials in the Washington Writing Archive is housed in the George Washington University Gelman Library. The Word Works is a member of the Community of Literary Magazines and Presses.

wordworksbooks.org

Other Word Works Books

Annik Adey-Babinski, *Okay Cool No Smoking Love Pony*
Karren L. Alenier, *From the Belly: Poets Respond to Gerturude Stein's Tender Buttons*
Karren L. Alenier, *Wandering on the Outside*
Emily August, *The Punishments Must Be a School*
Jennifer Barber, *The Sliding Boat Our Bodies Made*
Andrea Carter Brown, *September 12*
Willa Carroll, *Nerve Chorus*
Grace Cavalieri, *Creature Comforts / The Long Game: Poems Selected & New*
Abby Chew, *A Bear Approaches from the Sky*
Nadia Colburn, *The High Shelf*
Henry Crawford, *Binary Planet*
Barbara Goldberg, *Berta Broadfoot and Pepin the Short / Breaking & Entering: New and Selected Poems*
Akua Lezli Hope, *Them Gone*
Michael Klein, *The Early Minutes of Without: Poems Selected & New*
Deborah Kuan, *Women on the Moon*
Frannie Lindsay, *If Mercy*
Elaine Magarrell, *The Madness of Chefs*
Chloe Martinez, *Ten Thousand Selves*
Marilyn McCabe, *Glass Factory*
JoAnne McFarland, *Identifying the Body*
Leslie McGrath, *Feminists Are Passing from Our Lives*
Kevin McLellan, *Ornitheology*
Ron Mohring, *The Boy Who Reads in the Trees*
A. Molotkov, *Future Symptoms*
Ann Pelletier, *Letter That Never*
W.T. Pfefferle, *My Coolest Shirt*
Ayaz Pirani, *Happy You Are Here*
Robert Sargent, *Aspects of a Southern Story / A Woman from Memphis*
Roger Smith, *Radiation Machine Gun Funk*
Jeddie Sophonius, *Love & Sambal*
Julia Story, *Spinster for Hire*
Barbara Ungar, *After Naming the Animals*
Cheryl Clark Vermeulen, *They Can Take It Out*
Julie Marie Wade, *Skirted*
Miles Waggener, *Superstition Freeway*
Fritz Ward, *Tsunami Diorama*
Camille-Yvette Welsch, *The Four Ugliest Children in Christendom*
Amber West, *Hen & God*
Maceo Whitaker, *Narco Farm*

www.ingramcontent.com/pod-product-compliance
Lightning Source LLC
Chambersburg PA
CBHW020858160426
43192CB00007B/970